MORE THAN MONEY

Secrets of Excellence In The Market Place

FEMI ABIODUN

MORETHAN MONEY
Copyright © 2023

FEMI ABIODUN
ISBN 3107-1194-1576

Published by
ALPHASAGE

Cover Page By: Israel Odu +234 701 828 9712
Edited By: Teeinspire +234 703 260 7909

MORE
THAN
MONEY
Secrets of Excellence In The Market Place

MUCH ADO ABOUT CAPITAL

✌ MUCH ADO ABOUT CAPITAL... ✌

D ay by day, people get fresh business ideas but sadly, most of these ideas never see the light of day because a lot of folks blame their failure to start a business on the lack of money which contributes to the mortality rate of ideas being astonishingly high.

In fact, across the globe, countless people are stalling on their ideas, waiting for the perfect time and funds for execution. Some even believe they need to possess *"millions of dollars"* before they can launch out while others may have fantastic ideas but they do nothing about it until they see someone successfully executing exactly what they had intended to do with little or no capital.

Unfortunately, this notion of needing a huge amount of money to start a business has prevented countless people from executing their phenomenal ideas. Beyond doubt, money is needed to fund your idea and start a business, but I have both bad news and good news for you. The bad news is, indeed, money is needed to run a business but the good news is, money isn't all you need to start and succeed in business.

To put this in perspective, money is merely a factor necessary to run a business but it is not the ultimate need to start a business which translates into the fact that there are highly crucial factors other than money that are indispensable in kick-starting your business.

Though most people are loaded to do exploits, only a few attempt to open their package because they keep hiding under the guise of their excuses. When you ask people, *"why have you not started your business?"* Most people are likely to respond, *"I don't have capital."*

As a result, scores of fantastic business ideas were aborted. To say the least, organizations that ought to be employing job seekers and alleviating the high rate of unemployment never existed simply because the supposed visioner bought into the excuse of the *"lack of capital."* While it has become a norm for people to come up with excuses, these notions are merely excuses and shouldn't stop you from venturing into your desired business.

More Than Money is a timely book written to dismantle the limiting beliefs that prevent people from bringing their ideas to fruition and educate them about the genuine necessities or must-haves to start, sustain and succeed in business.

Femi Abiodun

chapter 1

SOCIAL CAPITAL

THE POWER OF RELATIONSHIPS

Humans are social animals and as such, have been given the gift of relationships, connections and collaboration but it behoves on us to fully optimize it. We are like living magnets designed to attract and connect with others as no man can be an island. The much-idolized capital we all (including entrepreneurs) long for, is actually hidden in the people in our lives.

Though only a few know this, you primarily need people to kick-start your business journey. How? To build a thriving business, you need to understand the operation and significance of these 3Fs in your life:

Ø   *Friends*
Ø   *Family*
Ø   *Foes*

FAMILY: This cannot be overemphasized as you will often need your family. They are the first set of relationships you will have and their love and support will be unconditional. Sometimes, they may be generous enough to give you the money, guidance and all the support you need to thrive in the business. In fact, in some cases, your first set of customers will be your family. Some may not give you money, but they will definitely plant the seed of encouragement you need to flourish in the business in you or they may offer you life-changing advice that will put you on the right path.

FRIENDS: Friends are also incredible support systems in life and your friends may also be your first set of clients in your business provided you have good ones. It is often said, *show me your friends and I* *will show you your future.* But more crucially is that associating with the right kind of friends will give you unlimited access to the information needed to start and succeed in business as many businesses have failed because the owners weren't privy to the right information due to their poor associations in form of friends while some failed to listen to the wise counsel from friends.

However, in getting counsel from friends, you must be very cautious because some of them will try to discourage you from fulfilling your dream of building a great business. Some may even be foes who disguise themselves as friends. This brings us to the last F. . .

FOES: This may sound like an oxymoron but for you to be successful, you need friends but to take it a notch higher, you need foes because they will inspire you to do your best if you do not lose courage. Simply put, *you need your foes to keep you at the edge of your toes.* Sometimes, in trying to counter or discourage you, your foes will unconsciously serve as fuel for you to put in your best as you wouldn't want to become an object of ridicule by them.

Yet, persecutions are simply raw materials for scaling high in the business world. As you wouldn't want your foes to rejoice over you, you will be brutally determined to succeed in business and life. Besides, you also need them to differentiate between the genuine and fake people in your life so you can deal with them accordingly.

Above all, we all need people to connect us from where we are going to where we want to be and as an entrepreneur, you need three sets of people in your life because they will determine how far your business will go. Furthermore, those who will assist you in the marketplace will appear in any of the three forms below;

1. **POINTER:** They *point* you in the direction and the right path to success. They will show you what to do, when to do it, where to do it, who and how to do it. They simply *point* out your place in destiny. If you do not have a *"pointer"* in your life, you will labour pointlessly. Sometimes, a pointer may not have what it takes to help you but they will <u>point</u> you in the direction of those who will eventually help you in the marketplace

2. **GUIDE:** They *guide* you through the nitty-gritty of your entrepreneurial pursuits. They do not check up on you to confirm if you succeeded or not. All they do is *guide* you through and give you the vital information sufficient for you to get results and move on.

3. **HAND-HOLDER:** They *show* you what to do and not just lead you in the marketplace but also take you by the hand to your place in destiny. They check up on you regularly to be sure you are doing the right thing. They teach, guide, mentor, coach, instruct and give you a shoulder to lean on. They let you know what you need to learn, relearn, and unlearn before you venture into business.

Ultimately, the impact of relationships is huge and non-negotiable. Here is a story narrated by a global thought leader that stresses the magnitude of relationships.

"A friend of mine was on the verge of being evicted from his house when they reached out to me. They needed to pay an outstanding rent of 400,000 naira to avoid being homeless at the time of our communication. I was travelling from Lagos to Akure in Nigeria (about 307 kilometres and while in transit, I put a call across to a few people and in less than 2 hours, the money was raised. That's what relationships can do."

Now consider this: when you are in distress, do you have the right contacts to rescue you? If your answer is No, you need a new set of people in your life. Let's assume you need 1,000 dollars to start your business. To put this in perspective, all you need is 10 people who can give you or lend you 100 dollars each. The question is, do you have such people in your life?

More so, you don't just need anyone but trustworthy people, after all, some people were lucky to have money but fell into the wrong hands and lost all they possessed eventually. Therefore, you must make a deliberate effort to build quality relationships. No matter how small or big your idea is, you need quality people to help you in execution. Your current neighbours, classmates and colleagues may be your destiny helper tomorrow so never look down on anyone.

When you walk out of people's lives, do not burn the bridge and make sure you've left your footprints in their hearts. Make it a norm to add value to everyone around you because you do not know whose help you will need in the future. Learn how to treat people with respect no matter what because your worst critic today may be your biggest client tomorrow. There is no permanent friend or foe in life.

If you are reading this and struggling to make headway in starting or building a profitable business, you may need to review your circle of influence. If your current tribe or community cannot help your business in any way, you need to start building new relationships with people of impact, influence, and affluence. Always surround yourself with people who inspire you, motivate you and place value on your life. For anyone who wants to go far in life and business, it is non-negotiable to be intentional about building the right relationships. And how do you build quality relationships? By giving value or helping other people. That's why it's being said, *"We rise by lifting others."*

The right relationships will open the right doors for you in the business world. Simply put, the kind of relationship you keep will determine if your lofty idea will flourish or not. Thus, be cautious about whom you allow into your life because eagles and chickens do not do business together. You can't afford to nurture any kind of relationship for the sake of it. You must be fully convinced that it will be beneficial to your life. Before you invest in any relationship, investigate it.

In addition, I am not of the opinion that some people are self-made as I strongly believe that whatever we achieve in life is a result of different inputs of different kinds of people we have met in our journey. However, for some people to support you in whatever you are doing, they must have seen your investment in their own lives which begs the following questions;

6

- How much are you contributing to the growth and development of the people around you?
- Are you charging a fee for what you could have done for people for free?
- Are you a bridge builder?
- How much honour do you give to people regardless of age, experience, and social class?
- How much do you genuinely care for the people around you?
- Is your connection with people relational or transactional?

The golden advice for anyone going into business is to deliberately build relationships. For people to truly care about your well-being and support your vision, they must Know you, Love you and Trust you. It is easy for people to know you and love you, but Trust is a scarce commodity in the world we live in.

One of the things that will make people trust you and help you optimize relationships is your Integrity. Integrity is not just doing the right thing but doing the right thing right. The money you need to launch out is not in heaven, it is inherent in people. Find below some acronyms used to further explain the power of relationships as a catalyst to fast-track whatever it is you are trying to achieve;

OPM: Other People's Money
OPT: Other People's Time
OPC: Other People's Connection
OPI: Other People's Influence
OPK: Other People's Knowledge
OPW: Other People's Wisdom

Before you set out in your business, make sure you surround yourself with quality people who have all the resources to help your business start and grow fast. Remember, a struggling man cannot help another struggling man. Only a man with enough blood can donate to other people who need blood. Below are more tips to help you build healthy relationships;

- Create value for the people around you. Don't live a parasitic life.
- Be courteous
- Be ready to assist even when it is not convenient for you
- Be helpful without expecting anything in return
- Be humble. Humility attracts.
- Mind how you relate with people especially those of lower status.
- Lend your help when people are at their lowest moment for posterity has a way of rewarding you.
- Have a strong and genuine empathy for people.
- Treat people well and they will reciprocate your goodwill and even pay it forward.
- Don't just connect with people, connect with progressive people.

Do not assume that all relationships will provide the support system you need to thrive in your business. Hence, there are 5 kinds of relationships you must identify;

1.   Relationship for a *reason*
2.   Relationship for a *season*
3.   Relationship for a *lesson*
4.   Relationship for a *blessing*
5.   Relationship for a *lifetime*

WISDOM NUGGETS

- You don't need the permission of anyone to succeed in business, but you need their collaboration.

- Honour is a delicious meal no one can reject. When you sow respect into other people's lives, you will reap honour.

- The man you abandoned like a rag in his dry season may be useful for you whenever it rains.

- If you give the right people a drop of water, they will turn it into an ocean. If you give the wrong people an ocean, they will dry it up.

- Until you give to people, you are not likely to receive from others.

- Favour from genuine people will add flavour to your labour.

- It is not stupidity when you take a deliberate effort to help people even if they have nothing to give in return.

- If you build relationships for the sake of personal gain, you will surely end up in pain.

- If you do not make deposits in the relationship bank, you cannot make withdrawals.

- Anyone can be a tourist in your life but not everyone deserves a permanent residence.

- Those who desire to collect from people do not make an impact like those who seek to connect with people.

- Your genuine connection with quality people will guarantee collections

- Blood is thicker than water is a timeless axiom. Do not ignore it.

chapter 2
MENTAL CAPITAL
THE ACUMEN AND KNOWLEDGE

D o not go ahead to begin a business you do not have basic knowledge about because it can be disastrous as every business requires in-depth information and knowledge to commence. Even if you outsource the business expertise required to build your business, you also need the know-how to sustain it as a lot of mental work is required to successfully run it and stand out.

Information is the most valuable asset in the human world. Therefore, access to valuable information will save an aspiring entrepreneur from unnecessary waste of time, energy, and resources. On the contrary, mistakes become inevitable when an entrepreneur lacks quality information.

Without mincing words, every serious entrepreneur must invest in quality research such as conducting a feasibility study to understand and gain mastery of the industry they are venturing into. A wise man once said, *"When you are ignorant about something, it is an invitation to learn."* My question is, *"how much do you know?"*

Mental capital provides you with the intellectual capacity to succeed. However, many start-ups have not been able to attract their desired investors because the proprietors cannot exhibit convincing knowledge about their business, yet they yearn for investors to fund their business. Make no mistake about it, no investor is ready to gamble with his or her investment.

But if you go ahead to start a business without adequate knowledge, you will be at the mercy of your competent staff especially those who may want to defraud your company realizing that they understand the business more than you. This equally applies to your customers who really know what they want and they may make a fool of you when you appear to be an amateur before them.

Another school of thought strongly believes that every budding entrepreneur must study the reason why some businesses failed even before they start theirs because by doing so, they will avoid the booby traps and danger zones in the course of building their own business. Simply put, if you plan to start a business soon, you need a thorough level of knowledge before you begin.

Read the biography of successful and failed businesses because the stories of successful businesses will inspire you to emulate their principles while that of the failed ones will ensure that you work smarter and harder to avoid common pitfalls in building a successful business. Failed business stories equip you with the insight that ensures you do not replicate their mistakes.

It is also noteworthy to state that the knowledge you acquire to start a business will not be the same as you need to sustain it. You need to upgrade your knowledge consistently as running a business requires that you open yourself to new vistas. You cannot build a business on residual knowledge or native intelligence because the world is dynamic and drastically progressing, and information moves at the speed of light. For this reason, you need to consistently upgrade your know-how to thrive in business.

There are, however, six (6) levels of learning;
1.   Ignorance
2.   Knowledge
3.   Skill

4.   Expertise
5.   Author
6.   Guru

Every business thrives on the discovery of new vista that births innovations and enhances competitive advantage. Today's new and biggest idea will be outdated tomorrow.

Therefore, there is a need for contemporary skills, dexterity and know-how in starting, building, and sustaining a business. The depth of mental capital at your disposal will enable you to develop a compelling Unique Selling Proposition (USP) that will separate you from your competitors and the saturated market.

Finally, how far your business will go is a function of your imagination. Before you start, how far do you foresee your business going? Your imagination is elastic and how far you can stretch it will determine how much you get from it.

More so, if you don't programme your mind for success, there is no way you can attract it. In other words, a wrong mindset will only produce a wrong business.

I have seen people go into business with an *ant* mindset, yet they want to build a mega business. How impossible! So, stretch your mind!

14

WISDOM NUGGETS

- You are likely to run into debt if you don't have depth in the business you are investing in.
- When you consistently ignore what you don't know, you will remain ignorant.
- If you build your business for the sake of the common culture, it will be devoured by the industry's *"vultures."*
- You cannot have a grasshopper mentality and build a mega business. You cannot be thinking like an ant and become a giant in your industry.

- You must first invest in the know-how of the business you intend to start before thinking of investing financially.

- As an entrepreneur, you must learn as if your knowledge is going out of fashion.

- The more you learn, the more you will earn.

chapter # 3

EMOTIONAL CAPITAL
THE STATE OF YOUR HEART

The task involved in running a business can be so herculean that we sometimes doubt ourselves and then depend on external validation or motivation but let me burst your bubble; you don't need external validation or encouragement before you start a business and if you are the type who craves for *sweet words* from people before you take deliberate steps, you will never get to your destination. You first and foremost need self-motivation to start.

Until you win the battle of the mind, never think of starting a business because some people will definitely condemn your dream in a way that would make you quit. Nonetheless, ships don't sink because of the water around them. They sink because of the water that gets into them. So, never allow people's negative opinions to dampen your spirit as you build your business venture. Sometimes, you may have doubts and that's normal but if you amplify that inner doubt, it will be evident to the people around you and the prospective customer you want to engage and it could pose a huge problem.

But be it as it may, the moment you set out to start your business, you will attract persecution, especially from those in your inner circle. Therefore, if you do not have a thick skin for criticism or *"despise the shame,"* do not even attempt to start a business. Put differently, if you are waiting to be encouraged by people other than yourself, you will not succeed in business.

As a matter of fact, every great entrepreneur at one point in time *despised the shame* and used mockery and persecution to fuel themselves to business success. Nevertheless, failure is inevitable in business and even in life. My question, however, is, *how will you handle failure when it shows up?* Will you *react* to the challenges or will you *respond* to them? I repeat! Do not kick-start a business if you are allergic to insults.

- What do you do when things do not work out as planned?
- Do you blame yourself, your family, others, the system or even the government?
- What do you do when your business is rejected when starting because it's inevitable?
- If you are not accustomed to hearing *"No"*, you cannot be an entrepreneur.

The fear of *"what will people say?"* is one of the major reasons why some people have not started their business but the truth is, other people's opinions do not matter if your conviction is right and if you have a habit of carrying your emotional baggage around, it's high time you dropped it if you intend to thrive in business. It all starts with the state of the mind. You cannot think small and build a mega business because there is a huge correlation between how you think and what you can achieve.

Simply put, no magic or miracle can make a small thinker build a global brand. Like an idea, a business is a seed and every seed will take ample time to germinate and grow. Yet, to germinate and grow, a seed must be nurtured. Consider the successful companies around you and you would realize that none of them was built overnight. That's why those who want instant gratification cannot build a lasting venture.

To round off, before you start, you ultimately need the *courage* to produce irresistible goods or services that will stand the test of time and cannot be refused.

- You need courage!
- You need the courage to be yourself.
- You need the courage to charge a premium for your goods/services.
- You need the courage to say "Yes" to what you want and go after it.
- You need the courage to say "No" to what you don't want
- You need the courage to hire the right staff.
- You need the courage to query and fire non-productive staff.
- You need the courage to not be sentimental.
- You need the courage to approach and attract high-paying customers or clients.
- You need the courage to confront bad customers or clients
- You need the courage to solve daunting problems
- You need the courage to embark on projects that are beyond you.
- You need the courage to ignore mockers.
- You need the courage to forge ahead even when the road is rough.
- You need the courage to do the right thing even when it is not convenient for you, or it is against public opinion.

WISDOM NUGGETS

- Other People's Opinions will not put food on your table.
- *"What will people say?"* will not pay your bills.
- The state of your mind will determine the stage you will attain in your business.
- *"I will get back to you"* has killed many ideas. Keep pushing and don't give up!
- To get the lion's share in your industry, you need a lion's heart.

chapter 4

SPIRITUAL CAPITAL

THE GOD FACTOR

Most people have lost huge businesses (sometimes their lives) due to the myopic belief that mere common sense (IQ), skills, commendable business plans and financial capital are just enough to run a business. How erroneous! Because it takes much more than these to excel in business. You may consider me to be biased but in every marketplace, there are gates and there are gatekeepers as well and in this chapter, I will be unravelling the mysteries about the power of prayers, faith and the importance of the supernatural in business.

For every business you are trying to build, there are mystical forces to contend with and how spiritually equipped you are will determine if you will win or fail in the marketplace as there are some secrets of the marketplace that are not available in the public domain. That's why they are called, *"secrets."* In fact, to get to the pinnacle of any industry, you need to dig further in the Spirit to access them because everything answers to the spirit (good or bad).

The crux is, every business has a spiritual dimension and it takes *spiritual intelligence* to thrive in the business world. Take this as a hoax at your peril but several business owners who also trivialized spiritual intelligence ended up losing their businesses because for as long as you venture into business, you have to call on God or some kind of gods as the Business sector is a war zone and going into the marketplace without being spiritually fortified is synonymous with going to a battle without a weapon. You become susceptible to tribulations.

Accordingly, spiritual intelligence remains a huge advantage in the marketplace and your spiritual capital will determine the answers you provide to the following questions;

➢ *Why do you want to start this business?*
➢ *Where do you go?*
➢ *Who do you partner with?*
➢ *When do you start?*
➢ *How to go about it?*
➢ *You must go before God to inquire.*

The book of Jeremiah 33:3 says, '*Call to me and I will answer you. I'll tell you marvellous and wondrous things that you could never figure out on your own.*' (The Message) In other words, secret things are only revealed in secret places. Therefore, it behoves you to devote more time to intense prayer, studying and quality meditation otherwise, it will be difficult to progress in the business. In fact, your business can only be safeguarded by your spirituality and these things may not be explainable as they are mystical.

Though this may seem weird, this is a true-life story to learn from; I worked in the Nigerian advertising industry for a couple of years and whenever a big brand wanted to change their advertising agency, they called for a pitch. Though these brands may sometimes not intend to change the incumbent advertising agency, they could call for a pitch to harvest fresh ideas or charge up the incumbent to avoid complacency even if they are doing excellently. However, clients may also call for a pitch for other reasons.

In this scenario, a pitch was organized and all interested agencies submitted their bids and were shortlisted and a representative of each agency was called up to make their presentation within the brevity of an allocated time. On this fateful day, the representative of a particular agency (who were favourites to win the contract) got to the conference room while all directors and stakeholders were seated and as he attempted to start pitching his well-prepared ideas, he got blank!

I mean, he could not utter any word as everyone waited including the stakeholders. The alarming thing was, everyone saw his lips moving but no one could hear him speak as his words mysteriously became audible. After several failed attempts, the organizers ran out of patience, believing he would only waste more time and he was asked to exit the room for the next agency.

More shocking is that the moment he stepped out of the room; he suddenly could speak audibly again and everyone heard him this time but alas, he had already lost out and his agency was snubbed. While people were astonished, only the spiritually sensitive could understand that the occurrence was diabolical. Hence, spiritual fortification in the marketplace is a no-brainer and every aspiring entrepreneur should focus on these four things to succeed:

1.   **CONSULT**

     Because the spiritual controls the physical, there is always a need for spiritual *consultations* in terms of prayer. Simply put, do not start a business until you have had profound spiritual *consultation* and still, never be complacent. Endeavour to ask the right questions in the place of prayer. Just as every successful organization spends a fortune on surveys, reports and research before they delve into any business, ensure that you invest time and effort in spiritual *consultation* for clear instruction and direction before you start a business.

2. **CONTEND**

You need to be equipped to *contend* and outsmart the forces in the marketplace because most of the difficulties you will encounter have spiritual undertones so you must live ready otherwise you will be consumed by the *"vampires"* in the industry. You cannot be a fingerling and successfully defeat the sharks. The spiritual muscle you have built over time is what will make you fit to *contend* with your competitors.

3. **CONQUER**

Even after you *consult* and *contend*, milestones can still not be achieved until you *conquer* your rivals in your industry. Yes! Without that, you can neither dominate nor be at the frontline in your industry. To *conquer*, you need a good niche, a unique selling point and revelatory knowledge to enhance your superiority in the industry and only if you have access to these business secrets will you attain lofty heights. However, these secrets can only be revealed to you in the place of your spiritual exercises.

4. **COLLECT**

It is often said, *"It takes the lion's heart to get the lion's share"* and until you become invincible in the marketplace, you cannot access the freebies and treasures in your industry. It is good to have a strong plan and strategy, but it is also essential that you claim what belongs to you in the prayer room. One of the strategies of the devil against your business will be to

25

instil the spirit of fear in you. Therefore, building your faith is non-negotiable so that you can overcome the crippling power of fear.

Ultimately, grace provides the opportunity to do exploits and it is a major currency we all need to excel in the marketplace.

WISDOM NUGGETS

- Strategy without adequate spiritual preparation will lead to tragedy
- Beyond the marketplace, your faith determines your fate in life.
- If you fail to nurture a strong spiritual culture, you will be devoured by the marketplace vulture.
- Scores of businesses have gone extinct because the founders neglected spiritual intelligence.
- In the marketplace, if you lack the unction to function, your business will be auctioned.
- In the business world, you are either operating in a secret cult or in the secret place.

chapter 5

PHYSICAL HEALTH CAPITAL
POWER, ABILITY AND AGILITY

Venturing into business without physical fitness is tantamount to embarking on a journey of no return because running a business entails vigour and stress and only the physically fit can deal with the daily strenuous tasks to achieve the ultimate goal. Physical fitness ensures that you feel good in your body, maintain a healthy weight, and utilize plenty of energy for both work and play and these can only be achieved by a healthy lifestyle.

Your body is an engine needed to effectively run your mind's vision of running a business. Money may buy you a good life but it cannot necessarily buy you impeccable health. Yet, it is startling to see many aspiring entrepreneurs and even the established ones chase financial goals at the expense of their health.

As a budding entrepreneur, let me ask you this rhetorical question, how far do you think you can go with rich financial capital but poor health? Another question; if you are to live for 100 years and you are given only one car to drive for a lifetime, how would you maintain that car?

Every aspiring and existing entrepreneur should understand that running a business comes with vigour and rigour, meaning, it could be physically and mentally demanding. For this reason, there is a need to judiciously take care of your body. In point of fact, one of the most stressful adventures is entrepreneurship. Therefore, anyone who wants to succeed in it should never take his or her health for granted.

No matter how intelligent, spiritual, sociable, and courageous you are, take care of your health before you consider starting a business because it is the only place you will live in. Your business may fail and you will still be fine but if your health fails, it is finished. Henceforth, take your health seriously by managing stress, eating well and exercising regularly. To stay healthy, here are some recommendations by experts;

➤   Regular body check-ups
➤   Regular exercise
➤   Watch what you eat and drink

As an entrepreneur, if you do not have routine fitness activities, you will not be able to do much in business.

Below are some reasons why every entrepreneur must remain fit;
*   Physically fit entrepreneurs are more agile and productive.
*   Physically fit entrepreneurs are more fortified to handle challenges.
    Physically fit entrepreneurs can easily explore their innate creativity.
*   Physically fit entrepreneurs experience lower levels of stress, anxiety, blood pressure and are at far lower risks of suffering common diseases.
*   Physically fit entrepreneurs are more confident and possess better self-esteem.

WISDOM NUGGETS

- In business and life, you cannot attain some feats if you are not physically fit.
- Your physical health is absolutely non-negotiable. You may negotiate other things but not your physical health.
- Just as you place a premium to maintain and maximize your assets, your health is a greater asset you must maintain and maximize.
- If you are financially rich but physically poor, you are still poor.
- What shall it profit a man to make all the monies in the world and lose his health?

chapter 6

FINANCIAL CAPITAL

MONEY IS A DEFENCE

Every potential and existing entrepreneur must be smart with money because it is crucial to make money but it is even more crucial to understand the language and code of it. This highlights the need for *financial intelligence*. However, most entrepreneurs are after money making but disregard this which can be disastrous. Without further ado, every aspiring entrepreneur must build a strong team of these financial experts;

- Accountants
- Bookkeepers
- Auditors
- Financial advisors
- Wealth Managers
- Tax consultants
- Risk managers

These experts are needed in your circle of influence to help you make informed decisions as they will aid your cash flow, help you to avoid many booby traps and spot opportunities you are blind or unfamiliar with.

With such experts on your team, your business to grow in leaps and bounds because they will provide you with timely advice that will save you costly mistakes. More so, loads of entrepreneurs struggle with expanding their businesses or diversifying as they invest in businesses they know little or nothing about. This is where these experts will come in handy.

Furthermore, below are some things to take note of to manage money effectively;

1. Be cautious in dealing with credit cards and loan facilities because they have the propensity to make you spend more.

2. Avoid getting involved in a lottery or ponzi scheme as they can ultimately ruin you financially.

3. Shun the habit of buying or procuring products or services that are not needed. For instance, buying a luxurious Rolls Royce, yacht, or recreational vehicle that is too expensive to maintain can ruin you.

4. Don't hire too many staff, particularly when you are just starting as it can drain your treasury.

5. Don't invest in a business you are not sure of, familiar with or any field you know little or nothing about. Do not also invest in what people are not buying or ready to buy.

6. Cut your day-to-day expenses which can affect your savings and cash flow.

7. You are not running a bank or finance house so, avoid giving out loans, especially to family and friends when your business is just starting or even thriving.

8. Curb your appetite for delayed gratification to enable you to manage your cash flow efficiently.

9. Do not play toil with your tax as it may later haunt you, especially in a structured economy. This is why you must have a tax consultant in your circle.

10. You must negotiate everything and make sure you reach a zone of a possible agreement to save money for your business. Do not be discouraged by the face value of a service or product you intend to buy. Negotiate! Negotiate!! Negotiate!!!

11. Gradual progression is better than delayed perfection so, avoid aiming at perfection for there will be times when you

make errors in trying to manage your cash flow. Thus, do not wallow in pain or self-pity. Always consider the risk and Return on Investment (ROI) carefully before you invest.

12. Avoid unnecessary borrowing and never spend the money you have not made (in profit)

13. If you do not have enough capital to buy the needed asset, you may lease or rent as it saves you from financial stress.

WISDOM NUGGETS

• In all your getting, get a team of financial experts who will hold you by the hand on how to make, manage and multiply your money.

• Cash flow makes the entire business flow

• Before you invest in any project, investigate.

• If you hire wrong people, your organization will not go higher.

• At every point, make sure your money is working for you and not against you.

• Never give up on the financial goals you set for your system.

• There will always be a time of abundance and scarcity.

chapter 7

CUSTOMER IS KING BUT YOU ARE THE KINGMAKER

I believe in the axiom; *"If you treat your customer well, he will tell his neighbours. But if you treat him badly, he will announce to his neighbourhood."* Take a moment to let this sink into your mind. Now, what does this mean to you? Remember that there is a huge difference between *"tell"* and *"announce."*

There is a need for you to know your customer absolutely before you go into a business. Now, get this straight! Whatever business you intend to do will not attract everyone's attention. I mean, not everybody will buy from you. This is the harsh reality in business you must know. Therefore, you need to know the exact age group, class and target of people you are meant to focus on and serve.

To succeed in business, you must have deep insights into your customers' needs, habits, behaviour, and traits. More importantly, you need to understand them individually because each customer will patronize you for different reasons. While some may be looking for the extraordinary benefits of your product, others may patronize you for emotional reasons or personal aggrandizement.

One principle that must guide your customer attraction strategy is the AIDA principle;

ATTENTION: You need the *attention* of your prospective customers. Thus, everything must be done to ensure their *attention* is colonized. This can be possible through compelling campaigns, storytelling, advertising or marketing communications.

INTEREST: Once the attention of your prospect is grabbed, *interest* becomes possible. However, there must be proper attraction and engagement before a prospect can ever develop an *interest* to patronize. Make them irresistible offers and give them a genuine reason to make a buying decision.

DESIRE: *Desire* comes when the target customer is fully persuaded that the product or service will solve problems for him beyond any reasonable doubt.

ACTION: This is a point where the customer finally decides to make a purchase or subscribe to a service. *Action* translates to purchase.

Until you get the above correct, you cannot attract the right customers. To aid you, the following questions must also be accurately answered before you launch out to give you clarity and avoid shadowboxing and waste of time and resources;

- ➢ Who are your customers?
- ➢ Where are they?
- ➢ Where do they live?
- ➢ Where is the market?
- ➢ What do they like or dislike?
- ➢ How much do they have to spend?
- ➢ How do they spend?
- ➢ Where do they spend?
- ➢ What is their language?
- ➢ What is their lifestyle?
- ➢ What is their belief system?
- ➢ And many more.

Every business needs to find accurate answers to these questions and come up with an impeccable customer experience service that would be tailored to meet the customer's DNA (Desire, Needs and Aspirations). Nevertheless, your interaction with customers will make them experience any of these four;

1.   Your service can make them MAD
2.   Your service can make them GLAD
3.   Your service can make them SAD
4.   Your service can make them SCARED

WISDOM NUGGETS

- Excellent customer service is synonymous with doing a money ritual
- No customer is absolutely loyal. Once they see a better service, they may likely leave.
- Your customer should be your biggest and most visible advertising billboards.
- When your customer is continually satisfied, he will make excuses for you even when things go wrong.
- It is good to win your customer's money, but it is better to win their hearts.
- While you consider your customer to be king, remember that you are the *kingmaker*.
  As a business entity, your point of *reference* is your point of *difference*.
- Never downplay the importance of referrals.
  Every feedback from your customer must be an input for your next strategy.

❧ FINAL WORDS ❧

Every king you admire today was once a crying baby. The crux is, life is in stages and no one ascends a throne from the womb. Therefore, start from square one. Start with what you have. Do something fast about your idea because you are not the only one with the vision.

Learn how to document and celebrate your little achievements as it will boost your confidence and will encourage you to do greater things. Do not let the big players in your industry intimidate you. When you do your research well and remain consistent, you will find your own unique niche. Keep learning and growing fast. Every time the sun rises is an opportunity to invent new things.

Do not be ashamed to crawl, and endure the walking stage because every flying aircraft was once on the ground. Never forget that growth takes time. This is why they say, capacity is built over time, not overnight. It may not take time to walk but it will take much more time to fly and soar.

Remember, money is extremely essential, but you need more than money to start and prosper in business!

Printed in Great Britain
by Amazon

29335675R00030